101 Ways
to Spoil
Your Grandchild

101 Ways to Spoil Your Grandchild

VICKI LANSKY

Illustrations by Rondi Collette

CONTEMPORARY BOOKS

Library of Congress Cataloging-in-Publication Data

Lansky, Vicki.
    101 ways to spoil your grandchild / Vicki Lansky ; illustrations by
Rondi Collette
       p.   cm.
     ISBN 0-8092-3231-6
     1. Grandparenting—Miscellanea.   I. Collette, Rondi.   II. Title.
HQ759.9.L35   1996
306.874'5—dc20   96-15774
                                                              CIP

Published by Contemporary Books
A division of NTC/Contemporary Publishing Group, Inc.
4255 West Touhy Avenue, Lincolnwood (Chicago), Illinois 60646-1975 U.S.A.
Copyright © 1996 by Vicki Lansky
Printed in the United States of America
International Standard Book Number: 0-8092-3231-6

18   17   16   15   14   13   12

Introduction

Usually I write from experience. The truth is I am not yet a grandmother. But I think I understand the magic. My sister is a grandmother six times over now, four of the women who work with me are grand-mothers, and several of my good friends recently became grandmothers. I've observed them all very carefully. Combine that with the fact that my own children are in their early twenties and starting to think about life partners themselves, and I think I have a vision of the experience of grandparenthood.

Our children grow up and turn out to be just folks. They aren't perfect, and we parents can see that better than others. But a baby—that's a different story. There is no history here. Just a clean slate, an opportunity to begin the dream again. We know that the deliciousness of youth is not forever. We have acquired the perspective that one gets only after having produced children who have reached adulthood. (Notice I did not say *maturity*— only adulthood.)

It's a clean slate for us, too. We do not have to be the people our own children remember. We can create a new history with our children's children. They change our vision of history and create new beginnings for us.

And of course the best part is that we can return these special little people to the loving hands of one or both of their parents after an hour, a day, or a week. What could be closer to perfection?

We can offer our grandchildren unconditional love, be a source of their roots, and be heard in ways that our own children can never hear us. If we choose, we can fill a need that can be filled by no one else. As has been said, we'll be remembered for the time (not the money) we give our grandchildren.

And as for our own children, a new relationship develops—sometimes overnight—as they become parents. Often this is the harder relationship to deal with. While we may see their becoming parents as an extension of our own lifeline, they need to lay claim to their parenthood as the beginning of theirs, a lifeline that is *apart* from us. We may feel that since our children are really extensions of us they will parent as we did. Prepare for disappointment! As much as we hate to admit it, parenting methods do change from generation to generation. (Remember how we all knew the best way, the latest theories, the best advice, etc.? Well, so do they.) Each generation is entitled to do it their way—even if it is "wrong." We were.

Advice given gratuitously—no matter how delicately put—usually sounds like criticism. And criticism creates hard feelings. Our children don't want to be parented. They want to parent—all by themselves. So we must learn to wait until we're asked for advice or to ask for permission to offer advice. Rejection of advice should be taken graciously—not personally.

Let your adult children, whether they live nearby or far away, know your baby-sitting parameters up front to head off negative feelings. This means letting them know, before they ask, how often or how long you're willing to do child care, at whose house, and whether you're available for emergency fill-ins. Discuss the fine points. Baby-sitting should not mean housework. Don't get compulsive. A daughter or daughter-in-law—or a son or son-in-law—may have a greater tolerance for your diapering variations than your laundering methods or your reorganization of the kitchen cabinets.

Support is what new parents need. Support is something we give with our hearts and our ears, not with unasked-for advice. My favorite story is of the grandmother who gives a baby gift to each of her friends as they become grandparents for the first time. With the baby gift that is to be passed along to the new parent she also includes a little wrapped gift for her adult friend, the new grandparent. It is a roll of transparent tape—a visible reminder of how important it is to keep one's lips sealed. (Now, will I remember this good advice when my time comes?)

Acknowledgments

Many thanks to these parents and grandparents who shared their ideas and insights:

Helen Brooks
Dawna Brown
Malinda Collins
April Donaldson
Jean Evans
Bonny Freese
Lillian Goldfine
Denise Harben

Joanne Healy
Pam Jarmon
Joyce Jones
Joy Knudson
Mary Louise Kutsch
Winnie Kuzara
Robyn Martin
Carolyn Mason

Eileen Pankow
Francie Paper
Connie Peters
Sandra Podergois
Chee Chee Posh
Bruce Resnick
Phoebe Resnick
Suzi Resnik

Kathryn Ring
Judy Ryan
Barbara Schiff
Tara Shannon
Dianne Skelly
Dorothy Skelly
Debbie Skinner
Theresa Thomas

Spoil your grandchildren! . . . with the parents' permission, of course. It's a grandparent's right—and responsibility—as well as a grandchild's expectation. Always say hello and good-bye with a hug and a kiss. Make it a point to spoil all the grandchildren equally.

Celebrate the birth of each grandchild with a very special gift. It can be a financial investment or something to be treasured, such as a passed down silver rattle or even a bottle of wine to be opened on the grandchild's twenty-first birthday.

Plant a tree upon the birth of each grandchild, and then take a picture of it each year to mark your grandchild's birthday. If your grandchild is nearby, the child can be in the picture, too.

Videotape some of your normal activities—getting into the car, cooking dinner, doing yard work, wrapping a gift—and send the tape to a grandchild. Alternate these tapes with ones in which you demonstrate a skill, such as teaching a magic trick or building a birdhouse. Ask your grandchild's parents to send tapes of your grandchild in return.

Look for one of those clever T-shirts that proclaim "If I Had Known Grandchildren Were So Much Fun, I Would Have Had Them First" and wear it when you're with your grandchild.
Or have a pair of shirts customized to delight your grandchild.

I'm Jennifer's Grandma!

I'm Jennifer's Grandma's Girl!

On your grandchild's birthday, send a card or note to your adult child at least once thanking him or her for making you a grandparent. It is sure to be shared with your grandchild.

CAUTION GRANDCHILD ON BOARD

If you love those precious grandchildren as much as you say you do, transport them in a car only when they're buckled up or in appropriate car seats. Buy, borrow, or rent one if you need to. (Remember, children under 40 pounds *must* be secured in car seats. It's the law!)

Before you throw it out, go through your junk mail with your grandchildren in mind. Often such mail contains stickers and items that can be colored or cut and pasted.

When the grandchildren are coming, check out an armload of age-appropriate books from your library. Get help from the librarian if you aren't sure what to select. If time permits, share the visit or return of the books with the kids. Consider getting your grandchild a library card to use during visits with you.

When did you last visit the zoo, a circus, or a fair or watch a parade? Let your grandchild be your ticket to go again—and again and again. A particular event can be an annual tradition you both look forward to.

Schedule regular sessions of "Granny School" or "Grandpa School" with one or more grandchildren—to do a craft project such as knitting or woodworking, to write a story together in ongoing chapters, or just to read together on topics of mutual interest.

If you see your grandchild weekly, choose a book to read aloud in installments. It might be one you enjoyed as a child or one selected from a book review you've read.

Enjoy everyday living experiences when you're together: wash dishes, fold laundry, or scrub the bathtub. (Parents usually see these as chores to be done quickly rather than as learning experiences.)

Use the holidays to share seasonal gifts or traditions that will be appreciated. Some ideas: a Halloween mask or a Christmas ornament you make together each year; a new pair of shoes each Easter or a Chinese New Year toy as a gift; a heart-shaped cookie baked for Valentine's Day.

Create a postcard collection for grandchildren by sending them one from every place you visit. Perhaps you can look forward to visiting some of these places together.

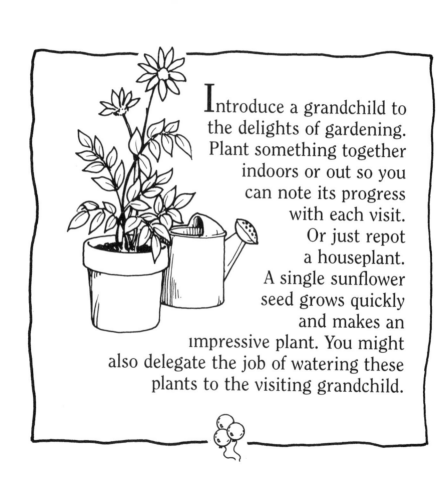

Introduce a grandchild to the delights of gardening. Plant something together indoors or out so you can note its progress with each visit. Or just repot a houseplant. A single sunflower seed grows quickly and makes an impressive plant. You might also delegate the job of watering these plants to the visiting grandchild.

Send letters to grandchildren whether they live nearby or far away. Print the words for new readers. Draw a message or paste magazine cut-outs for a very young child. Short notes are best. Send a greeting card if you have nothing special to write about. Don't let having nothing to say stop you!

Grandma Andora
312 Hickory
Pleaston Town
New.

Ashley James
431 Dreams St.
Monroe, Michi...

Dear Ashley,
The flowers
we planted
are very pretty.
Thank you for
all your help.
What have you
been doing in
school? I'll be

Use a file folder or a large envelope for each grandchild to store papers and photos no longer on display. Occasionally go through these mementos with the child.

Use them to start a scrapbook or photo album. The kids will love to watch themselves grow on the pages of the album.

Before calling your grandchild (especially if it's a long-distance call), jot down some notes about what you want to ask or talk about. Be prepared to bear the responsibility for keeping your phone conversation going.

√ Cub Scouts
√ candy sale
cience test
bike
r blades
com ter

Save different-size boxes for your grandchildren to build playhouses or forts when they come to your home. The boxes can be scored, folded, and stored without taking up much space.

Set up a regular phone date with a grandchild that's convenient for both parents and grandparents. Check into getting a personal 800 number that

grandchildren can use to call you if you live far away. Occasionally talk to grandchildren over the phone *without* asking to speak to Mom or Dad.

Grandchildren love birthday presents from their grandparents, particularly if they are *not* clothes. Ask for suggestions from your children. If stumped, one crisp dollar bill for each year of age will be appreciated by younger and (especially) older kids—even though the amount won't be a surprise.

Occasionally send a letter or card that involves an activity. Create a connect-the-dots activity using numbers or letters or make up a crossword puzzle using words that are part of your grandchild's life—a street name, a favorite color, a food, and so on.

Don't succumb to competitive grandparenting. Put out the welcome mat to the other grandparents. Don't hesitate to encourage your grandchildren to call them from your house, even when it's not a local call!

Tape coins to greeting cards. Children love peeling the coins off the card, whether to spend or to save.

Read to your grandchildren in the morning
in bed at your home or theirs. Comics,
books, and photo albums are all great. Offer
to read aloud to grandchildren even after
they are old enough to read to themselves.

At the end of a visit to your grandchild's home, hide a little something—a stick of gum, a quarter, a note—under the pillow, in the sock drawer, anywhere. With your final good-bye or when you next speak to your grandchild on the phone, give clues to the location of the surprise.

Once your grandchildren are beyond bibs and high chairs, put on an occasional formal dinner party. Let the children help you set the dining room table with good china, silver, cloth napkins, and candles or flowers, and then treat them as your special dinner guests. It's fun and an etiquette lesson as well.

Try to spend more time with a grandchild whose parents are going through separation and divorce, especially during that first year. Let the parents know that your only interest is keeping a bond with your grandchild. No grandparent should miss being close to a grandchild because a son or daughter left a marriage, and no child should lose a grandparent.

Be sure to offer all grandchildren your verbal "grandparents' seal of approval." Letting them know you think they are terrific at all ages is wonderful for their self-esteem and offers great feelings of security in an uncertain world.

The Hug of Approval...

Whether you're nearby or far away, be sure there are recent photos of you for grandchildren to see in their own home. Send a suitably framed photo of yourself or yourselves for display in your grandchild's bedroom. And do send one to each grandchild—even in the same household.

Autograph the photo while you're at it!

Bake cookies for or with your grandchild. It's a cliché that's worth every calorie. Premade refrigerated cookie dough makes very good treats if time or talent is limited.

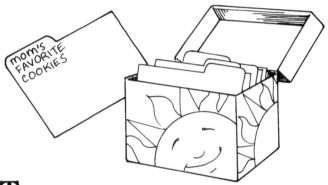

Teach kids how to prepare some simple dishes their parents liked as children. Write down these recipes for them to take home.

Older kids may enjoy the art of garnishing. Check the library or a bookstore for books that show how to create items like cucumber boats, food flowers, and other decorations.

Tell grandchildren stories about their parents. They love to hear that Mom and Dad used to do something just the way they do, especially something silly. You'll probably recall events your children have forgotten (or so they'll claim) that your grandchildren will find fascinating.

Try to teach grandchildren skills their parents may not take the time to teach them—sewing, knitting, crocheting, woodcrafts, fishing, gardening.

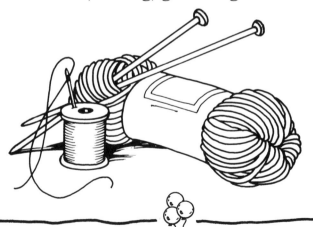

Teach a small child simple songs you can sing while together or on the phone. Share your favorite music.

Encourage the kids to dance to it, keep the beat, and conduct an imaginary orchestra. Older children will often be interested in going to concerts with you if they are familiar with various kinds of music.

Be creative with your letters. Write to your extended family in the form of a newsletter, adding information and maybe photos of each member's activities as well as your own. Or write messages on balloons that you deflate and mail. Play chess or another game by mail. Send news clippings of interest to older grandchildren.

Surprise a grandchild with a "just because" gift for no special occasion to arrive by mail—even if you live nearby. A coupon for a burger or an ice cream cone from a franchise eatery is easy and appreciated.

Before a visit from an out-of-town grandchild, write expressing your delight about the upcoming visit. Ask for suggestions of what you should do together.

Create a few small rituals that can be repeated at every visit. Leave a small present to be found in a drawer, or maybe go out for an ice cream cone at the same spot each visit.

Draw a simple family tree to help each grandchild understand family relationships. If possible, paste small pictures of folks next to their names. Here is one way to diagram the concept for an old-enough-to-understand grandchild.

Remember your grandchildren especially on Valentine's Day. Giving cards, a store-bought giant Valentine cookie, a heart-shaped red balloon, or anything else heart-shaped is a wonderful way to send Valentine love.

Devise a secret handshake with your grandchild.

Teach your grandchild one new joke at each visit or phone call. "Knock-knock" jokes are good for years. If necessary, consult your library for books to widen your repertoire.

Try a "Joker's Wild" party at which each person must contribute two new jokes to the conversation!

Join the recycling "clean up your world" movement with your grandchildren. Pick a yard, park, or public area to go to with at least one grandchild and a couple of trash bags (one to be used for cans and bottles that can be recycled). This activity can last for ten minutes to an hour, depending on the ages and attention spans of the children.

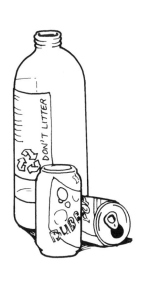

If you are fortunate enough, take a grandchild to visit a great-grandparent as part of your time together to help strengthen family relationships.

Take a trip with a grandchild of eight or older, be it a few days at Disneyland or a half-day fishing trip. Special intergenerational programs are available through organizations such as Elderhostel. Look into agencies that specialize in off-the-beaten-track grandparent/grandchild trips. Let your grandchild be part of the planning process.

Give your grandchildren gifts of their parent's favorite childhood toys that you've saved. Both children and their parents are usually delighted with them.

Keep a box of saved old clothes, handbags, shoes, hats, and the like for visiting grandchildren to play "dress-up." Periodically add things to the box so there is always something new there.

Encourage grandchildren who live far away to write to you by sending them stamped and addressed postcards. You might even create a form letter for an older child to fill in the blanks.

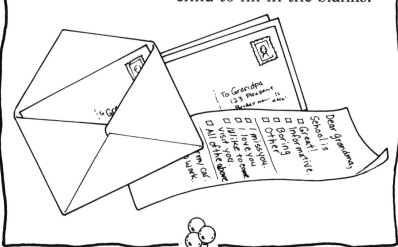

NOW PLAYING

ADMIT ONE
the Wind in the Willows
SAT. MATINEE

Presented by
The Children's Theater

Invest in season tickets to your local children's theater group to share with one or more grandchildren.

Start a collection of interest to a grandchild, such as bells, postcards, miniature cats, or other figurines, whistles, and so forth. Then add to it when you travel, at holiday time, or when you're shopping together.

Be sympathetic if a visiting grandchild is homesick—it doesn't mean you're not loved. Try another visit when the child is older or when circumstances are different, but only when the child feels ready for it.

Allowing older grandchildren to use you as a listening post for complaints may be the most special gift you can give. Acknowledge their feelings and enjoy knowing you've let them vent those feelings without taking sides or acting. Above all, keep these sessions confidential.

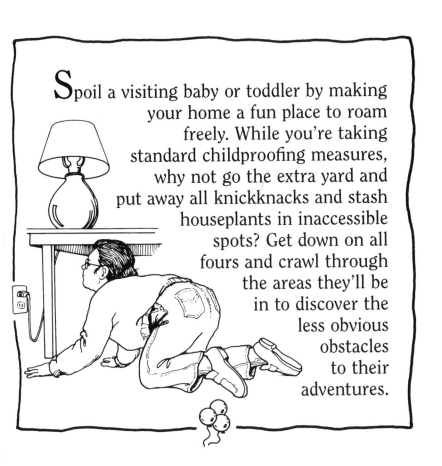

Spoil a visiting baby or toddler by making your home a fun place to roam freely. While you're taking standard childproofing measures, why not go the extra yard and put away all knickknacks and stash houseplants in inaccessible spots? Get down on all fours and crawl through the areas they'll be in to discover the less obvious obstacles to their adventures.

Send or bring along on a visit old pictures of your children as kids. Grandchildren love seeing Mom and Dad when they were little. If you're not prepared to pass these photos along, photocopy some for a grandchild to keep, color, or cut up.

Initiate bedtime prayers with your grandchild if that is a tradition his or her parents are comfortable with.

Try to think of outdoor traditions you can pass on—making a clover chain, playing "loves me, loves me not" with daisy petals, or making a finger whistle with a blade of grass.

Write a birthday letter to your gran
recalling what was special about this la
year, including new accomplishments an
shared experiences.

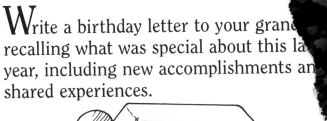

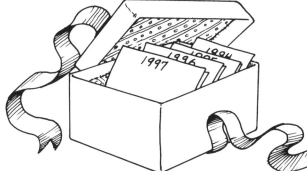

Do this each year and make a copy to add to
a keepsake box for each grandchild.

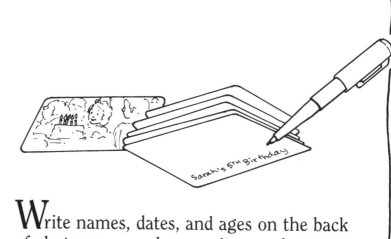

Write names, dates, and ages on the back of photos you send or receive—to keep your history clear. Memories fade more quickly than pictures.

If you consistently use one perfume or after-shave lotion, put a drop of it on a cotton ball and use it to make scented letters or gifts that your grandchild will associate with you.

Keep a photo album for each child and fill it with photos sent to you.

Keep suitable snacks on hand when grandchildren are visiting. Remember that *suitable* means familiar foods, not what you think they *should* eat or develop a taste for.

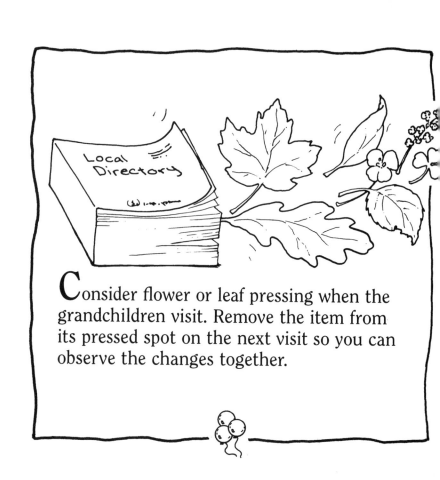

Consider flower or leaf pressing when the grandchildren visit. Remove the item from its pressed spot on the next visit so you can observe the changes together.

Take a grandchild out to lunch or breakfast occasionally. Eating out together is very grown up, and good one-on-one time.

MENU

Invite an older grandchild to bring a good friend along occasionally when visiting you.

Send or bring new bathtub toys for small children from time to time. (You're sure to be remembered during the daily bath!)

Encourage your grandchildren to take photos. Send or give them disposable cameras. Include the cost of developing or ask them to send the film back to you. This plan ensures you'll get to see what they're up to!

Play or learn to play popular games like Go Fish, Candy Land, Sorry!, and Uno.

Children are usually happy to teach a willing participant the rules!

Ask parents for ideas about what videos to rent and watch with your grandchildren. Have a home movie night with a rented video and view with fresh popcorn.

Sleeping Beauty

Charlotte's Web

Take a grandchild on one of your short business trips or, if retired, visit the place where you used to work. For instance, if you had a government job in Washington, D.C., your experience would add an extra dimension to a sight-seeing trip there.

R̲emember when feeding small children that creatively presented foods are often eaten first.

Try egg sailboats, cheese slices shaped with a cookie cutter, and food faces made by putting eyes and noses on most anything.

Let your grandchildren pick out something tangible they would like from your possessions to specify in your will. Or, perhaps better, give them an heirloom or household object now and enjoy watching their pleasure.

School-age children are fascinated by secret codes. Teach them Morse code or a simple number code (A = 1, B = 2), and then use it to send short messages back and forth.

A ·—	K —·—	U ··—
B —···	L ·—··	V ···—
C —·—·	M ——	W ·——
D —··	N —·	X —··—
E ·	O ———	Y —·——
F ··—·	P ·——·	Z ——··
G ——·	Q ———·—	STOP ·—·—·—
H ····	R ·—·	comma ——··——
I ··	S ···	Question Mark ··——··
J ·———	T —	

Start a college savings fund of one kind or another for a grandchild and add to it on birthdays and holidays. Any part of the child's education it pays for is a gift beyond measure.

If a grandchild visits you frequently, take out a subscription to a children's magazine for him or her to look forward to and then take home.

Ask Mom or Dad if the magazine is age or interest appropriate. (*Sesame Street Magazine* subscriptions for the two-to-six-year-old set come with a free bonus of *Sesame Street Parent's Magazine*, which you might enjoy, too.)

Check to see if you can volunteer as a room parent at school if your grandchild's parents' work schedules do not accommodate that kind of commitment.

Keep some toys and books for grandchildren to play with and read when they visit. Store them in a special closet or drawer so the children know where to look when they arrive. Add a new item once in a while for extra interest.

KEEP OUT!
FOR GRANDKIDS ONLY!

Let grandchildren help decorate your home for the holidays.

"My grandmother's too busy spoiling me right now to talk. So please just leave your name and phone number and she'll call you later."

Let your grandchild record your outgoing message on your answering machine.

Create a book featuring your grandchild as part of the story.

It can be handwritten or computer generated. The art can be your own, or you can use pictures cut from a magazine.

Keep track of your grandchild's activity schedule so you can ask appropriate questions and get more than yes and no answers.

Make or buy your first grandchild a christening or naming outfit that can be passed on to successive grandchildren and become a family heirloom. Check with the parent first to be sure the tradition isn't already in place.

Be studiously impartial. Never compare your grandchildren to each other. It's normal to have a special bond with one child or another, but showing favoritism to one child is hurtful to children and their parents.

Preserve your grandchild's adorable sayings in a quote book you can give him or her years later. Parents often forget or don't take the time to record such gems, especially after the first child.

For the young reader, start your own Grandparents' Book-of-the-Month Club, where you send one book a month (maybe in a series) to your grandchild.

APRIL'S BOOK OF THE MONTH LOVE GRANDMA

The Cat in the Hat
Green Eggs and Ham
One Fish, Two Fish

Help explain the symbols of your religious traditions to grandchildren. Dual-faith grandchildren can be helped to understand that ethical values, social responsibility, and belief in a higher power are shared by all religions.

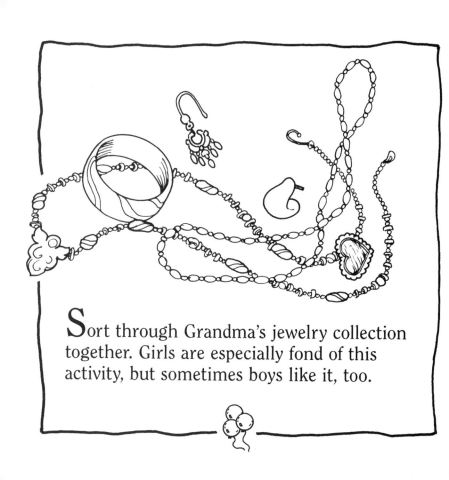

Sort through Grandma's jewelry collection together. Girls are especially fond of this activity, but sometimes boys like it, too.

Share a secret. Maybe each time you are together you and your granddaughter put on red nail polish that you remove before she returns home, or you and your grandson make a surprise gift for his mom or dad. Conspire with older grandchildren so they can take their parents out to dinner or buy a birthday present, with you providing the cash or gift certificate.

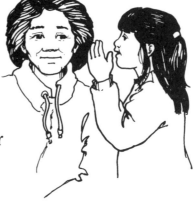

Keep track of growing grandchildren by using a doorjamb or wall space to mark their height. Include name, age, and year on a piece of invisible tape you can write on. Use different-color pens for different children.

Eric 10
4/96

Eric 9
2/95

Lee 8½
10/96
Lee 8
4/96
Lee 7
2/95

Ashley 5
4/96

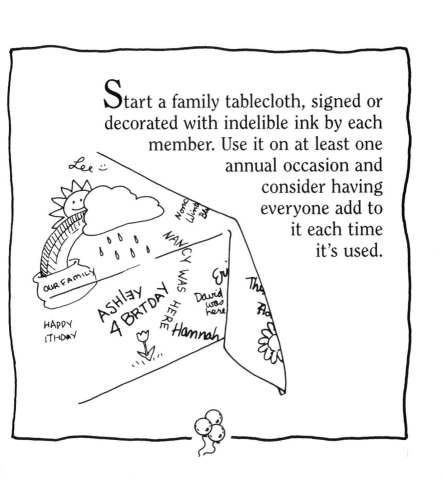

Start a family tablecloth, signed or decorated with indelible ink by each member. Use it on at least one annual occasion and consider having everyone add to it each time it's used.

The first Sunday in September after Labor Day is Grandparents Day. If your children don't invite you to  do something with their kids, ask them!

GRANDCHILDREN
ALL OF THE
FUN
AND NONE OF THE
WORK!

Ask to see grandchildren's report cards.

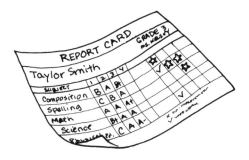

Grandparents can help motivate children by fussing over good report cards and leaving constructive criticism to their parents.

Watch a sunset with a grandchild and listen to his or her thoughts.

Set up jigsaw puzzles that can be worked during the entire length of an out-of-town grandchild's visit. Or keep a puzzle set up for nearby grandchildren.

If possible, set aside at least one day or half a day each year to spend alone with each grandchild. Let the grandchild help you plan your shared day and do something you both enjoy.

If your household and your grandchild's both have computers equipped with modems and on-line service, use e-mail to keep in touch. And if you have access to a fax (and the kids do too), use it for one-page correspondence, seeing their schoolwork, report cards, and the like.

Invite same-age grandchildren over for a slumber party.

Organize
a family reunion so that
grandchildren get to know and share
experiences with extended family members.

Feed the ducks
(or the pigeons or
the fish) together.

To remain a special and well-loved grandparent, remember that advice that is not asked for is advice that should *not* be given.

The rule of thumb is "Bite your tongue!"

Books by Vicki Lansky

- Feed Me I'm Yours
- The Taming of the CANDY Monster
- Practical Parenting Tips for the First Five Years
- Games Babies Play
- Getting Your Child to Sleep
- Birthday Parties
- Welcoming Your Second Baby
- A New Baby at KoKo Bear's House
- Toilet Training
- Dear Babysitter Handbook
- Baby Proofing Basics • Trouble-Free Travel with Children • 101 Ways to Tell Your Child "I Love You" • 101 Ways to Make Your Child Feel Special • 101 Ways to Be a Special Dad • 101 Ways to Be a Special Mom • 101 Ways to Spoil Your Grandchild • Vicki Lansky's Divorce Book for Parents plus • Another Use for...101 Common Household Items • Baking Soda: Over 500 Uses • Transparent Tape: Over 350 Uses • and other titles

To order any of the above, or to receive a free catalog of all Vicki Lansky's books, call 1-800-255-3379 or write to:
Practical Parenting, Dept SGC, Deephaven, MN 55391-3275